Charles K. Field

Four-Leaved Clover

Being Stanford rhymes

Charles K. Field

Four-Leaved Clover
Being Stanford rhymes

ISBN/EAN: 9783337422769

Printed in Europe, USA, Canada, Australia, Japan

Cover: Foto ©Thomas Meinert / pixelio.de

More available books at **www.hansebooks.com**

FOUR-LEAVED CLOVER

BEING

STANFORD RHYMES

BY

CAROLUS AGER

(CHARLES KELLOGG FIELD, '95)

REPRINTED FROM THE STUDENT PUBLICATIONS, WITH SUNDRY
TRUTHFUL PICTURINGS, BY DONALD HUME FRY, '95,
AND AN APOLOGY, BY DAVID STARR JORDAN

Second Edition

SAN FRANCISCO
WILLIAM DOXEY
1896

*Of the two hundred and fifty copies
making the second edition of this book, this
is Number* 121

Press of C. A. Murdock & Co.

This little book may perhaps be dear
  To some who tenderly recall
The Stanford grapes, and the Mayfield beer,
  And the girls of Roble Hall.

DEDICATION.

My four-leaved clover groweth not
Upon Parnassus steep,
But on the Palo Alto hills
Where Stanford poppies sleep;

And though these song-weeds cluster not
Beside the Muses' well,
The Spring-filled Lagunita Lake
Perchance may do as well;

No brilliant bloom, but rooted deep
In Stanford loyalty,
Their still small voice may speak to those
Who share that love with me,

Who once within a cloistered place
Were college mates of mine,
In clover there for four sweet years
That bore the stamp divine;

Then, though this lyre have but two strings,
One Love, the other Beer,
I calmly dedicate them both
To every Pioneer.

A FELLOW can be young but once. So it is with a university. It is a royal experience when one's own youth and that of his university come together. All the more glorious is it when, with all this, one has the gift of song, if he does not take it too seriously, and when the university has the charm of beauty and the glow of hope. The highest value of tradition lies in the making of it, and the rhymes of Carolus Ager are part of the traditions of Leland Stanford Junior University. To those of us who were part of the four precious pioneer years of the university, these rhymes have a value beyond that given by any literary clever-

ness they may possess. They are "original docu-
ments" in our academic history. Each one recalls
a day which the now sober and decorous University will never see again. And it may be in
place to remind the still more sober and decorous
public, to whom these rhymes are not addressed,
that they are not to be taken too literally. Love
and wine in youth are metaphors only. "The color
of life is red," cardinal red, according to our theory,
and the Zinfandel has the same color. The red
wine of these rhymes is not Zinfandel; it contains
no alcohol, nor has it ever crossed "the Mayfield
bar." It is the flow of young life. So, too, with
Love. It is not the serious, fateful thing it seems,
"once you have come to forty years." It is a
symbol only, the emblem of "the great thing
always to come, who knows?" But those who
have been once young understand all this, and the
others, let us hope, will never hear of Carolus
Ager.

David Starr Jordan

SUMMARY.

He who was here with us is now no more;
   Across the river he has wandered far;
I wonder if upon the other shore
   We'll meet again as at the Mayfield bar.

               —From the Sequoia.

CONTENTS.

The sea gives her shells to the shingle,
The earth gives her streams to the sea ;
They are many, but my gift is single,—
My verses, the first-fruits of me :
Some sang to me dreaming in class-time,
And truant in hand as in tongue ;
For the youngest were born of boy's pastime,
The eldest are young.
         —SWINBURNE.

13

CONTENTS.

SECOND LEAF — THE SOPHOMORE: —

14

CONTENTS.

15

CONTENTS.

16

CONTENTS.

17

I made myself a poet in the place,
  And blithely sang of college life and ways,
The pleasure of the undergraduate pace,
  And all the joy between the holidays;
No care spoke ever in my careless song,
  From graver strains I kept my pipe apart,
And played the upper notes; ah, was it wrong
  To dream my music reached the student heart?

Upon a day one said, with kind intent:
  " Why sing forever of these trivial things
For better music was your piping meant;
  Will you confess such earth-restricted wings?
Strike some Byronic chord, sublime and deep,
  Find in ethereal flight the upper air,
And speak to us some word that we may keep
  Within our hearts and ever treasure there!"

Then, with one pang for wasted hours, I gave
  Another meaning to my faltering lay,
And sang of Life and Pain, an early grave,
  Hope and Despair, and Love that lives alway:
But when I listened for an echoing heart,
  I saw all other lips with laughter curl,
And heard them whisper jestingly apart,
  " He's got it bad, poor fool; we know the girl!"

FIRST LEAF

THE FRESHMAN

THE DAYS OF '91.

DEAR chum of mine, do you recall,
    When college had begun,
The gladness of that glorious fall,
    And how we spent the "mon"?
The days of cheer, the days of beer,
    The days of '91.

Dear maid of mine, do you recall,
    When first my heart you won,
There were no lights in Roble Hall,
    But, oh, such loads of fun?
The days of dark, the days of spark,
    The days of '91.

Dear major prof, do you recall
    The night, at set of sun,
We met, when each had made his haul
    Where vineyard pathways run?

THE DAYS OF '91.

The days of scrapes, the days of grapes,
    The days of '91.

Dear Class of '95, when all
    The four years' thread is spun,
The Freshman follies we recall
    We would not have undone;
Those days when youth came seeking truth,
    The days of '91.

COMING THRO' THE QUAD.

(THE PIONEER VERSE.)

F a body meet a body
    Coming thro' the Quad,—
If a body see a body,
    Can't a body nod?
Ev'ry lassie has her laddie,
E'en tho' seeking knowledge;
Stanford girls are much like those
In any other college.

If a body meet a body
    On the cement walk,—
If a body greet a body,
    Can't she stop and talk?
Sweeter far is conversation
    In the open air
Than on Fridays, in the parlor,
    When the matron's there!

22

OH, LET US WEEP FOR ROBLE!

h, let us weep for Roble! He is dead.
With cruel wheels the locomotive sped,
And both the burnished rails were blotched with red.
Poor dog!

Full many tears celestial eyes have shed,
And many maiden hearts bereaved have bled;
He will no more with angel-food be fed,—
Poor dog!

Then let us weep for Roble; he is dead.
The earth is heaped upon his final bed,
The green of spring-time sprouts above his head.
Poor dog!

A LAMENT FOR THE DEAR DEPARTED.

His step is gentle, his voice is low,
　　His manner meek as Moses;
I watch him softly come and go,
At work about the room, and know
　　His murmured words obeisance show,
Each move his awe discloses.

My rugs need shaking much, but he
　　Perhaps has not been taught it,
And so, one morning, pleasantly
I say this must no longer be,—
And find, alas! his awe of me
　　Is not the thing I thought it.

Though this has failed, I bring to mind
　　The good that coin can do one;
And so a hoarded "half" I find,
And hand him it, with aspect kind,

24

And, by his dazzling smile made blind,
   Fancy my way the true one.

Another Jap this morning came
   To fix my room up neatly;
And I presume it were a shame
To think the vanished one to blame,
Because — a curse upon his name! —
   He shook the room completely.

HONOR AMONG THIEVES.

HORSEMAN rides through the autumn
  night,
  (The grapes are heavy upon the
   vine,) —
He searches the left, and he scans
  the right,
And his eyes are keen in the cold moonlight,
 (For grapes devoured shall never make wine).

There crouches a student among the leaves,
 (The grapes are purple upon the vine,) —
But many a shadow the eye deceives,
And the guard rides on in his quest for thieves,
 (And grapes devoured shall never make wine).

Somebody crawls through the yielding fence,
 (The grapes are trembling upon the vine,) —
His Faculty whiskers give evidence

HONOR AMONG THIEVES.

Of unimpeachable eminence,
(But grapes devoured shall never make wine).

There in the shadow the two have met,
(The grapes are fewer upon the vine,) —
The sudden start that one does n't forget,
The recognition that 's sadder yet,
(And grapes devoured shall never make wine).

A clasp of hands in the hush of night,
(The grapes are missing upon the vine,) —
And somebody's lips are pledged so tight
That to somebody else they need never recite,
(And grapes devoured shall never make wine.)

DANGER!

HEY were strolling slow together
    Where the oak-leaves scattered lay;
In the sky, with sunset burning,
Floated many a flaming feather
    Fallen from the wings of day;
And the eastern hills stood yearning
    For the daylight fled away,—
Yearning for the vanished bright-time,
Shivering, naked, in the night-time,
    Till the mist rose from the bay.

In the quiet of the gloaming
    Slowly up the path they strayed,
Sophomore and Roble maiden;
Love, on vagrant pinions roaming
    Where the last long sunbeams played,
Winged an arrow mischief-laden,—
    Wounded deeply man and maid;

28

And they wandered ever slower,
While the sun sank low and lower,
  And the hills grew dim with shade.

Ah, for them the days are over
  Which in earnest work were spent;
Study must give place to dreaming,
Student has been changed to lover,
  Cupid is omnipotent!
Single-hearted ones, esteeming
  Logic more than sentiment,
Oh, beware of woodland rambles!
Flowering paths have hidden brambles,
  Safer far is plain cement.

EVENING ON THE CAMPUS.

EHIND a screen of western hills
 The sunset color fades to night;
Along the arching corridors
 Long shadows steal with footsteps
  light.
The banners of the day are furled;
 Thro' darkening space the twilight creeps
And smooths the forehead of the world
 Until he sleeps.

The oak-trees closer draw their hoods;
 A bird, belated, wings his dim,
Uncertain flight, and far above
 A star looks down and laughs at him;
The sky and mountains melt in one;
 Tall gum-trees range their ranks around;
The white walk marks its length upon
 The velvet ground.

EVENING ON THE CAMPUS.

From out the dusk the chimney points,
    Like guiding finger to the skies;
Down drops the curtain of the night,
    And all the plain in darkness lies,
When, as the college buildings seem
    To lose their form in shapeless mass,
The lights shine out as poppies gleam
    Amid the grass.

FATE.

I TOOK my books the other day,
    And studied in the Quad, alone;
But no professor passed that way,
I was n't called on the next day,
    That work was never known.

Up on the road beside the brook,
    One little hour we two beguiled;
I never looked inside a book,
But I met each prof whose work I took,
    And when I flunked, he smiled.

"THE HEAVENS ARE TELLING."

As I came over from Berkeley town,
    The sun in the west went slowly
        down,
    And all around, when the day
        was old,
The waves were gaudy with blue and gold.

The sun sank into the west away,
The colors faded from off the bay;
The waves grew dark, but overhead
The whole sky gloried in Stanford red!

"GUTER ALTER WEIN."

HEN, as a Freshman, I began
    To try the German speech,
I studied with a learned man
    Who knew the way to teach,
And, being an American,
    Was not beyond my reach.

He used continually the phrase,
    "Guter alter Wein,"
In showing me the devious ways
    That adjectives decline;
I wondered, in those guileless days,
    Why he so liked the line.

Ah, days of pastimes innocent!
    The other sports that are!
When my allowance never went
    Over the Mayfield bar,

Nor in my months' accounts I sent
    Such wash-bills home to Pa;

Ere our vocabularies grew
    Until I could divine
The meaning hid to earlier view
    In "guter alter Wein";
Until "studieren," "schlaffen," too,
    Were words not found in mine.

Unlearned the lesson of the lights,
    To go out at half-past ten,
And never know the time o' nights
    That I got in again;
I never failed to count the flights
    Of stairs correctly, then.

A Soph to-day, and wiser grown
    Along another line
Than German, my first year has shown
    The teacher's method fine;
There is no tongue-inspirer known
    Like "guter alter Wein"!

METAMORPHOSIS.

DEAR maid, but yesterday
    You passed along a shaded way;
    Filled were your arms with maiden-
        hair
And poppies warm; against your face
The light fern found a resting-place,
But more than flower or fern I thought you fair.

    Ah! that was yesterday.
    Your window ledge is wondrous gay
With green and gold; and you are there;
    But poison-oak upon your face
    Has found a second blooming-place,
And flower and fern, dear maid, are far more fair.

BARBARA'S LULLABY.

ULLABY,
    The night is nigh,
  Low and slow the herons fly;
    Sleep and rest,
    In the west
All the sunset fires die.

    Down canyons steep
    The white fogs creep
And blanket all the pine-trees deep;
    Through the grass
    Wind-songs pass
While the night-capped poppies sleep.

    Hush thee, dear!
    The dark is near,
All the oak-trees disappear;
    Dim bats fly,—
    Then lullaby,
The red lights blossom,— the night is here.

THE PIONEERS.

WEALTH of old tradition marks
     The other Universities,
Stories of great men gone before,
     But no such things as these
Could ever set our hearts aflame
Like that first year
That gave our glorious class its name
     Of Pioneer.

The college world was all before
     Us where to choose our place of rest,
And Sophomore stock was low, and lived
     By sufferance at best;
The other yells died out with shame
     When "Zah! Zah! Zeer!"
Made all the echoing Quad proclaim
     The Pioneer.

Then, with our war-paint we profaned
　　The dignity of ancient trees,
And with our magic numeral awed
　　The aborigines;
In sundry ways we let them know
　　We were right here,
And just what deference they must show
　　The Pioneer.

'T was then that in Encina Hall
　　The Roble maidens ate,
And we, though Freshman hunger gnawed
　　At us, were glad to wait;
For as they passed along the hall
　　The fact was clear
Each maiden had among us all
　　Her Pioneer.

We 've watched three other classes through
　　Their Freshman years since we were
　　　　there,

But somehow everything since then
    Has worn a different air;
No other days could be the same,
    None half so dear
As those that gave our class its name
    Of Pioneer!

SECOND LEAF

THE SOPHOMORE

IN MEMORY OF RICHARD ALBRECHT.

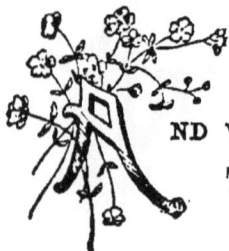

ND when you fell asleep, they said
  The good die young. Dear college
    friend!
We who are left have sometime read
  A sweet philosophy, that is to lend
Us comfort now that you are dead.

Life is a sleep, the poets say,
  A slow forgetting of the light
Shining from home upon our way;
  Ah, happy one, ere you had lost it quite,
God woke you, saying, "It is Day!"

TWO WINDOWS.

OPENED my window at sunset,
    And close to the sill I stood.
In the shadowy grass each poppy
    Had put on a pointed hood,
And over me far I saw the star
That comes with the sleep of things;
The last bird dreamed in her hidden nest,
Yet I heard the sound of wings!

I have watched the warm lights blossom,
    Like poppies that bloom at night;
These have faded away in the darkness,
    And only the stars are bright;
But I am still by the window-sill,
    Though all the day-world sleeps,
For the distant lamp of a midnight witch
    Over the oak-tree peeps.

43

A HERO.

OUT into the mud and the wet he goes,
    My hero, tall and strong;
Under his jersey the muscle shows,
And, Samson-like, his dark hair grows
    Delightfully thick and long.

Out from his feet the black mud flies,
    His jacket is far from white;
Bother these boys with their dapper ties!
Who come and compel me to turn my eyes
    Away from a nobler sight.

The hills are red with the western sun,
    The twilight comes like a dream;
But until the practice work is done
I strain my eyes for his every run,
    And I know he will make the team!

44

A HERO.

I envy the fellow who keeps his cap,
  With so little appreciation,
While I stroll back with a soft-tongued chap
Whose muscles I know are n't worth a rap,
  And whose hair is an imitation.

A SONG IN SEASON.

H, the rain!
    The buttercups overflow,
And out on the hill again
    The yellow violets grow.

Oh, the rain!
    And the loving mud to pass!
The 'bus waits long for the train,
    And the prof is late to his class.

Oh, the rain!
    When the bamboo bends to the rim,
And a girl and a hurricane
    Are waging a battle grim.

Oh, the rain!
    At the last sweet bell defied,
With one umbrella for twain,
    And a sidewalk two planks wide.

46

THE SECRET OF TWO.

E came to the Quad in a sweater,
The dude of Encina Hall;
The rest of us wondered whether
The skies were about to fall;
For the whole crowd put together,
In dressing, he beat us all.

Oh, the look on his love as he met her,
The gaze of the prof in class!
Transformed was the youth æsthetic,—
What wonder had come to pass?
Was he going to turn athletic,
This priest of the Flat-iron and Glass?

But one in the crowd knew better,
One soul, unconsulted and still,
Who held in his grim possession
A brown paper bundle, until
This gem of æsthetic expression
Should pay up his laundry bill.

47

MEMORIES.

No, my boy, you cannot please me
    With your cultivated choir;
Go yourself, but do not tease me
    From my place beside the fire;
For my heart is back at college
    While I dream here in the
        dark,
And I fancy I hear Shirley
    Asking us, "Who built de ark?"

Get some pretty girl to go, sir;
    They enjoy that sort of thing;
There was one I used to know, sir,
    When the quartet used to sing;
And when we went walking, later,
    You could count on one remark,—
"Isn't Mr. Baker funny
    When he asks, 'Who built de ark?'"

Give it up, my boy; I'm clinging
  To the songs of a dead day;
There are other voices singing
  In the firelight, and I pray,
When we meet in the hereafter,
  They will give us one good lark,—
And we all may answer Shirley,
  "Brudder Noah built de ark!"

RELAPSE.

STUDY Evolution,
    And hear the teacher tell
How we have all developed
    From an isolated cell;

And in the examination
    Some fellows make it plain
Their principles will bring them
    To the starting-point again.

WARNING.

AIDENS, when near the museum,
  Hush your confidential love,
Lest you teach a fatal habit
  To the statues up above;
For reflect, what dreadful discord,
  Think, what awful anger-blasts
Would be stirred up, if those statues
Ever got to "trading lasts"!

APOSTROPHE.

ou may talk of all the places
  Where you 've gone to eat
    your fill—
The Creamerie and Wilson's,
Maison Riche and Palace Grill:
They are magic names no longer,—
  You can tell it by my looks;
For I sing the German Baker,
  And the new French Cooks.

In the spring a young man's fancy
  Lightly turns to thoughts of love,
So they say; there are exceptions,
  Like myself, as I can prove;
For let all the other fellows
  Feast on love in pleasant nooks,
But give me the German Baker,
  And the new French Cooks.

Now, I don't go much on aliens,
  As a rule; but, if you please,
Don't restrict the immigration
  Of such charming men as these;
And instead of giving wealthy
  Girls to titled foreign crooks,
Let us swap for German Bakers,
  Or for good French Cooks.

I am longing less for mother
  Than I was not long ago,
And my weary way is brightened
  With a blessing, and I know
That the good Recording Angel,
  When he figures up his books,
Won't forget the German Baker
  And the two French Cooks.

STRATEGY.

"SOME, Cupid kills with arrows,
  Some, with traps;"
But this spring the little rascal
  Found, perhaps,
That he needed both to slay me;
  So he laid a cunning snare
On the hillside, and he hid it
  In a lot of maidenhair;
And I doubt not he is laughing
  At the joke,
For he made his arrows out of
  Poison-oak.

A SONG FOR HILDA.

WHERE the sunshine warm is sleeping
 When the noon is still,
See the baby-blue-eyes peeping
 From the grassy hill.
All day long the great Sun passes
 Through the sky above;
Baby-blue-eyes from the grasses
 Smile at him they love.

When the drowsy Sun is sinking
 Deep into the west,
See the baby-blue-eyes blinking,—
 It is time for rest;
And the Lady Moon when beaming
 On the darkened hill,
Finds the baby-blue-eyes dreaming
 Of the sunlight still.

A QUESTION OF COLOR.

MAIDEN dear, your eyes are blue,
   The glint of gold is in all your
      hair;
   But never may I to those colors
      two
Be loyal, although I must own them fair.
Still, beauty, though it bloom like yours,
   Is only transient after all;
Virtues are strong while love endures,
   And they in you are cardinal!

THIRD LEAF

THE JUNIOR

THE RIVALS.

HERE 's such a racket round my
    room!
  The fellow under me
Has frequent fits of frightful
    gloom,
  In which condition he
Upon a 'cello wails as though
It were the voice of one below
  Where souls in torment be.

A man who plays the cornet shrill
  Is quartered overhead;
Its strident voice is never still,—
  I swear he plays in bed;
But when he tackles "Robin Hood,"
And plays it like a dirge, I would
  That one of us were dead!

THE RIVALS.

There is a poor asthmatic flute
    That wheezes on my left.
If some fine day the heartless brute
    Should be of it bereft,
The record-angel, I dare think,
Would write me up in colored ink,
    And love me for the theft.

A singer dwells upon my right,
    Last but by no means least,
Who celebrates in song each night
    Some sweetheart now deceased;
And though his grief may be profound,
His upper notes, it seems, would sound
    More musical if greased.

What have I done, that these should join
    To make my fortune worse?
Is there no way, for love or coin,
    To rid me of the curse?
The happiest day that dawns for me

Shall be the one on which I see
　　The noisy flock disperse;

For though within my room alone
　　For hours I have stayed
And practiced on my big trombone,
　　It's lost time, I'm afraid,—
The racket round my room is such
I really cannot tell how much
　　Improvement I have made.

AT STUDY-TIME.

T study-time the white lamp
      throws
    Its light on many a page
      sublime,
    Where many a master's im-
      age glows,
At study time.

Yet evermore, through prose or rhyme,
  One sweet thought buds and gently grows
Full-flushed as roses in their prime.

At length, unread my books I close,—
  Ah, let them go! too sweet the crime
To think on thee, forgetting those
    At study-time.

LELAND STANFORD.

SWEET rest to thee and thine,
    illustrious head,
      Sweet rest and deep,
Where we have laid thee,
    after all is said,
      In granite-guarded sleep;
With that stern silence of long ages dead,
  The sphinxes vigil keep.

Not yet, strong heart, into that hush of stone
    Comes perfect peace;
Still waiting stands the third place open thrown,
    Unrest can only cease
When from the sorrow she endures alone
    One other finds release.

Sweet rest to thee and thine; in calm content
    Sleep quietly;

LELAND STANFORD.

More than a granite tomb the monument
    That ever stands to thee,
The gratitude of our great continent
    Thine immortality.

THE IDEAL CO-ED.

(WRITTEN TO MUSIC.)

THE ideal co-ed is a thing of books,
    A creature of brain entirely,
    With stooping shoulders and stu-
        dious looks,
    She digs all day and half the night;
People say she is wondrous bright,
But her figure's an awful sight!
Her thoughts are deep in the classic past,
She only thinks of A. B. at last;
    She has fled this world and its masculine charms,
    And a refuge found in Minerva's arms.

Now, the kind of co-ed that I describe
    Is a co-ed seen very rarely;
The real co-ed's a thing of grace,
With dainty figure and winsome face;
    She walks and rides, and she cuts, mon Dieu!

But every professor lets her through;
For her each year is a round of joy,
A. B. means nothing if not "A Boy,"
   And you and I must yield to her charms,
   And take the place of Minerva's arms.

DRINKING SONG.

(WRITTEN TO MUSIC.)

WE'LL go down the road to the Lit-
tle Vendome
When the stars are shining
bright,
And we'll fill up our glasses
and never go home
Through all the livelong night;
We'll drink, drink, drink, with laughter
free,
A toast to our University.

But the night must pass,
And there comes, alas!
A dark-brown taste in the morning;
O fill up your glasses — don't be a dig! —
Who cares a fig
If his head *is* big?

66

DRINKING SONG.

And what care we so long as we drink till
the dawning?

But next day in recitation
Oh! how hard to keep awake;
Raging thirst without cessation,
All one grand headache!
Ah! ha, ha, ha, ha!
What though sadly we may suffer,
What though suspicious be our looks,
Every student is a bluffer,—
We will sleep behind our books.

Come then, drink, with laughter free,
Drink to the University!
All too swiftly each year passes,
College life is wondrous fair —
Up then, boys, and fill your glasses,
Drink to the days that know no care.

Then fill up the glass to the sparkling brim
And drink until we fall;

Whoever can drink it we've welcome for him
    Beneath the redwood tall;
We'll drink, drink, drink, with laughter free,
Beneath the stately Palo Alto tree.

    Though the night must pass,
    And there comes, alas!
A world of woe in the morning,
We'll fill up our glasses — the man's a dig
    Who cares a fig
    If his head is big,—
So what care we so long as we drink till the
    dawning?

FALSE LIGHTS.

I HAVE a little attic room
    That looks upon the Row,
My head professor's clover lawn
    Grows grudgingly below,
And he can watch my study-lamp
Until to bed I go.

So with incentive such as this
    I trim my studious light,
And far into the short-wicked hours
    My window-square is bright,
And my professor knows he need
    Not ask me to recite.

Then sweetly let my beacon burn,
    And my professor smile,
Although between my light and me
    There lies a darkened mile;
My signal-lamp is trimmed, and I
    In Mayfield all the while!

69

MY LITTLE MAYFIELD GIRL.

(WRITTEN TO MUSIC.)

ost every one loves a co-ed —
  Some fellows love two or three,—
But among all the girls on the
  campus
    There is n't one in it with me,
For 'way down the road by the Brewery
  Lives one who sets me in a whirl,
While helping her Ma make tamales,—
  My little Mayfield girl.

  My pearl is a Mayfield girl,
    She 's all the world to me;
  She 's in it with any of the girls on
    the Quad,
    Though swagger and swell they be;
  At Dornberger's Hall, oh, she kills
    them all,
    As waltzing together we twirl,

No co-ed is in it with her for a
    minute,—
  My little Mayfield girl.

She never comes up to the classes,
  Or lectures or chapel at all,
But when there's a fifty-cent party
  I meet her at Dornberger's Hall;
Then I move in the Mayfield "400"
  And round in the lancers we whirl,—
I wonder she never gets dizzy,
  My little Mayfield girl!

  My pearl is a Mayfield girl,
    None is so sweet as she;
  Fred is forgotten, and Patsy, as well,—
    She makes the town for me;
  Then let all the rest of the boys go west,
    Where Roble sets young heads awhirl,
  But the shrine where I'm priest lies away
    to the east
  With my little Mayfield girl.

71

IN MEMORY OF LOUIS DONALD McLAINE.

WATCHED with one who heard, as in
in a dream,
The surging of far waters grow
apace;
The mist that rises from the nearer
brink
Settled in chilly damp upon his face;
There came a gentle color to the sky,
I saw the stars melt into morning air,—
A little yet he knew my ministry,
And then the river crept between us there.

When I had closed his eyes, a wonder came;
Another watcher bent above the place
Of my dead friend; dark, terrible, the shape
Bent over him, I could not see its face;
And then it turned to me; all heaven shown
From that calm brow, those eyes serenely
clear,

IN MEMORY OF LOUIS DONALD McLAINE.

Death left me with the body there alone,
 And witness me, I have not shed one tear.

*   *   *   *   *

One year ago this time he went away,—
 One year of struggle, ended in the spring;
Not all the shadow of our loss can hide
 The promise sweet that speaks in every thing;
Out of the underworld of clinging earth
 Freed nature finds the light.   We may not weep
Aloud for him; this season of new birth
 Hushes the murmur of our grief to sleep

A TOAST.

HERE's to the Freshman, all verdant
and gay,
Here 's to the Soph and his folly,
Here 's to the Senior afraid of next
May,
And here 's to the Junior so jolly;
Let the toast pass,
Drink to the Class,—
Her glory shall be our excuse for the glass.

Here 's to the Class that is leader in all,—
Long may she prosper and thrive, boys!
Then fill up your glasses and drink at my call
The glory of old Ninety-five, boys;
Let the toast pass,
Drink to the Class,—
Her glory shall be our excuse for the glass.

FOURTH LEAF

THE SENIOR

75

REUNION.

HE sun is warm upon the palms,
    The stately bamboos nod
As though they felt the freshened life
    That stirs within the Quad,
This happy time of meeting, when
    We greet so joyously
The voices that we hear again,
    The faces that we see.

But while this gladness fills the air
    A shadow steals our way,
Darkens the shining green and dims
    The brightness of the day;
The fellowship that cheered us then
    And now no more may be,
The hand we may not clasp again,
    The face we may not see.

REUNION.

Some day, perhaps, a sun may shine
    Where shadow is not known,
Where no such hungry thought as haunts
    To-day this echoing stone
Shall ever sadden meeting when
    We keep, eternally,
The voices that we hear again,
    The faces that we see.

A FRIEND IN NEED.

Come hither, little Freshman,
    And sit upon my knee,
And let me give you pointers on
    The University —
Some friendly words of warning,
    To guide you in a land
Whose ways are full of mystery
    And hard to understand.

No doubt the different teachers
    In whose kind care you prepped
Have told you many a fairy tale
    Which you as truth have kept,—
How college-life means struggle
    For intellectual ends,—
Vain theories, as you soon will find,
    Since you and I are friends.

A FRIEND IN NEED.

My boy, the world is moving,
  The old ideas outgrown,
And we must leave such ancient souls
  To fossilize alone.
Our battle with the brain is
  By no means what you dream;
The hardest thing you 'll have to do
  Will be to make the team.

Study your head professor
  More than the books you buy;
The proper study of mankind
  Is man, you know,— so try.
Fathom his favorite hobby,
  Some hidden crank unearth,—
Whether it 's books or babies, just
  Work it for all it 's worth.

When suddenly you find you 're
  Encompassed round about
By men of whose affection deep
  You hardly dare· to doubt,

Whose grasp, so firm and cordial,
  Pulls you this way and that,
Be not puffed up, but recognize
  The mystic signs of "Frat."

The girls who wait in ambush
  Along these cloistered ways —
Fear not, they will not care to frown
  Upon your Freshman days;
Take them on walks, to lectures,
  (When these are free, I mean),
And when the annual hops come round
  Then get a city queen.

One's Freshman year, young fellow,
  Is all too short and sweet;
To him we yield one precious boon, —
  The privilege to treat.
He may indulge in beer-feeds
  Uncriticised, although
There should be upper-classmen there,
  To give it tone, you know.

Oh, by the way, my money
   This month has been delayed;
You have n't got a V to spare
   Me, have you, till I 'm paid?
Ah, thanks! don't lend too often.
   It 's lucky you 've got me,
Old man, to give you pointers on
   The University.

THE PROF'S LITTLE GIRL.

HE comes to the Quad when her
Ladyship pleases,
And loiters at will in the sun
and the shade;
As free from the burden of work
as the breezes
That play with the bamboo is this little maid.
The tongues of the bells as they beat out the
morning
Like mad in their echoing cases may whirl
Till they weary of calling her,— all their sharp
warning
Is lost on the ear of the prof's little girl.

With a scarred-over heart that is old in the knowl-
edge
Of all the maneuvers and snares of the Hall,
Grown wary of traps in its four years at college,
And able at last to keep clear of them all,—

THE PROF'S LITTLE GIRL.

Oh, what am I doing away from my classes
    With a little blue eye and a brown little curl?
Ah me! fast again, and each precious hour passes
    In slavery sweet to the prof's little girl.

She makes me a horse, and I mind her direction,
    Though it takes me o'er many a Faculty green;
I'm pledged to the cause of her pussy's protection
    From ghouls of the Lab and the horrors they
        mean;
I pose as the sire of a draggled rag dolly
    Who owns the astonishing title of Pearl;—
And I have forgotten that all this is folly,
    So potent the charm of the prof's little girl!

Yet, spite of each sacrifice made to impress her,
    She smiles on my rival. Oh, vengeance I'd gain!
But he wears the same name as my major professor,
    And so in his graces I have to remain;
And when she trots off with this juvenile lover,
    Leaving me and the cat and the doll in a whirl,
It's pitiful truly for us to discover
    The signs of her sex in the prof's little girl.

MIZPAH.

VER the hills and far away,
  With marvelous muscles and
    wonderful hair,
  The team has stolen for secret
    play
Over the hills and far away,
  And only themselves know where.

Out on the oval a silence reigns,
  The stealing shadows are all alone;
Somewhere else each champion trains,
And all unwatched his muscle strains
  In some retreat unknown.

And we, who can only watch and cheer
  At nightly practice, must wait and dream
Of that mighty day that draws so near,
And, hovering still between hope and fear,
  Bet on our vanished team.

84

But when they come (ah! the days are few),
The Haight-street campers shall yield the day,
And the vanquished wearers of gold and blue
Shall fold their tents, as the Arabs do,
And silently steal away.

FOUR VALENTINES.

To-morrow is the day for valentines;
 Then let me leave my thesis for
  a space,
 Lower the lamplight on these
  weary lines,
 And dream a little in the shadowed place.
In my three years at college, I have named
 My Valentine and kept the season thrice;
The jolly saint himself is to be blamed
 If I have never had the same one twice.

In Freshman days, with all about me strange,
 And home's sweet halo shining on my way,
My heart had never known the sense of change,
 And one dear face was with me day by day;
So, when the time was here, I wrote my verse
 And drew the heart and arrow up above,
And, happy in the thought I might do worse,
 I sent it off to Mother with my love.

When I had felt the thrill of Sophomore days,
    My thoughts were given to a dainty maid
At college with me, and in woodland ways
    And quiet music-rooms my court I paid.
But, with my Junior dignity, I chose
    My Queen abroad, within the city's glare,
Forgot the violet for the gayer rose,
    And lost my heart and pocket-money there.

Saint Valentine, those days were long ago;
    Your power is lost upon this penitent,
For, with my Senior gravity, I know
    That life means more than your light sen-
            timent.
And yet, this once your day shall have from me
    Some of the old observance, though I scoff;
My thesis waits,—my Valentine shall be
    The old-maid sister of my major prof.

GOD'S ACRE.

H, so pure the white syringas!
　　Oh, so sweet the lilac bloom
　In the Arboretum growing
　　Near a granite tomb!
By the arching pepper-branches
Let us tender silence keep;
We have come into God's Acre
Where the children sleep.

In the trees the quail are calling
　　To the rabbits at their play,
While the little birds, unknowing,
　　Sing their lives away;
In the night-time through the branches
　　Wistfully the young stars peep,
But, with all these playmates round them,
　　Still the children sleep.

Once within that leafy shelter
  Some one hid herself, to rest,
With another little dreamer
  Folded to her breast;
And a sense of consolation
  Stealeth unto them that weep,
While that mother-heart lies sleeping
  Where the children sleep.

Year by year the Christmas berries
  Redden in the quiet air,—
Year by year the vineyard changes,
  Buds and ripens there;
We give place to other faces,
  But the years' relentless sweep
Cometh not into God's Acre
  Where the children sleep.

THE BALLAD OF WOODSIDE FIELD.

OME, gather round, ye merry men
 Who live within the Hall;
The feast is done, the door is shut,
 Then gather, gentles all,
And hearken to a tale of six,
 And what did them befall.

Now, Sir Adolphus was a Knight
 Of mickle might to see;
He hailed from off the frozen shore
 Of Northern Germany;
And no one in the brazen band
 Was half so bold as he.

His fists were iron-clad in strength;
 His arms were made of brawn;
Along Encina's reverent halls
 He walked with splendid scorn,
And blew his own horn valiantly
 From eve to dewy morn.

Then up rose wily Billinoles
    And listened to the strain;
The sound of Sir Adolphus' horn
    Gave him a subtle
        pain,
He vowed unto his
        patron saint
    It should not blow again.

He hied him up the winding stair,
    Up to the eastern tower,
Where dwelt the doughty warrior, Milt,
    A knight of dreaded power,
Whose fists to many a reckless foe
    Had brought his passing hour.

Sir Milt reclined within his hall,
    His pipe was in his hand;
He filled it from a casket near
    That bore the "Old Bull" brand.
The dust upon his books was deep;
    (You yoemen understand).

The wily Billinoles stepped in
    And softly locked the door;
With hellish art he argued there,—
    Ten minutes 't was or more,—
Until Sir Milt was pledged to wade
    In Sir Adolphus' gore.

Then up rose Billinoles again
        And hied him forth in
           glee;
        Adown the hall he sped as
           though
        Upon the track was he;
        The baleful light within his
           eyes
        Was dreadful for to see.

"Now, Sir Adolphus, hark ye well,
    Encina's bravest knight;
The bold Sir Milt has challenged thee
    To meet in bloody fight.

Up, then, and battle for thy fame,
    And Heaven defend the right!"

The Lord Gambrinus swore an oath:
    "By Adderson," quoth he,
"And every other evil power
    That blasts the land or sea,
I'll make this upstart bite the dust
    Ere he be done with me!

"Go get thee to the Earl of Jeff;
    Borrow a glove or two
And cast them at the feet of Milt,
    My high defiance, too,—
Or may all Roble cease to smile
    At me, as now they do!"

Oh, who can tell from words alone
    What lieth in the heart?
No sooner did the gleeful Bill
    Upon his way depart,
Than Sir Adolphus showed himself
    A man of boundless art.

Up to Sir Milt he made his way
  And pressed a novel suit,
Which was that they should pull the leg
  Of Billinoles so cute,
And give to him through all the world
  The lasting name of "Fruit."

Bright dawned the day on Woodside town;
  The lists they were prepared;
The swelling muscles of the knights
  Were to the sunlight bared.
Now listen, merry men, and hear
  Of how the heroes fared.

Sly Billinoles was there, and Vann,
  And a Scot of equal worth.
They turned away their evil eyes
  To hide their godless mirth;
(But Heaven took away from them
  Their mortgage on the earth).

Now would they brook no more delay,
  But bade the foemen stand.

They rubbed them down and faced them there
 Upon the good green land;
But both Adolphus and Sir Milt
 Showed woeful lack of sand.

Nor this nor that had been arranged
 As they would have it done;
Each hemmed and hawed, and so delayed
 To meet the other one,
Till Vann and Billinoles were tired
 And sweating in the sun.

But now at last they take their stand
 Within the oft-changed lists;
Up in the glad spring air they raise
 Their murder-dealing fists, —
When suddenly there comes a cry,
 And every one desists.

A cloud of dust, a frantic form
 Coming at breakneck speed,
Whose lightning rate the watchers know
 Bespeaks an urgent need:

It is the great Frazicrius
Upon his iron steed!

With gasping sides he wildly speaks:
  "For love of life, no more!
King David hath got on to this,
  And all your days are o'er,
If on this day the Woodside green
  Be stained with student gore."

This said, he fainted where he stood,
  And when in time brought to,
The gathering of valiant men
  Discreetly then withdrew.

The plot had failed, and three of them
  Were indigo in hue.

Down to the Redwood market-place
  They made a quick retreat;
Where Billinoles did set them up
  With sundry things to eat,
And all the dough that he could raise
  Was swallowed in the treat.

Now, all ye merry men, who hear
  The story of this scrap,
Remember oft the trapper falls
  Into his own sly trap:
It is not always whom we fool,
  That later wear the chap.

TO WALTER CAMP.

OOD-BY, until we meet again,
　　Thrice - honored friend from
　　　　Mother Yale!
　　Under whose stirring generalship
　　　　No team can ever fail.
We keep the hope that you will guide
　　Our course thro' many another fall;
Good-by! take with you on your way
　　The blessing of us all.

A THANKSGIVING TOAST.

NE of the team for the whole four years;
   Ah, what a record that!
Strongest and best of the Pioneers,
   Fill me a glass to "Phat."
Drink with me to his health again;
   This is no toast to sip;
Here's to the captain whose loyal men
   Saved us the championship!

Ninety-five, this is our triumph hour,
   Never again to be;
But when at length our boasted power
   Fades into memory,
Still in the hearts of us all shall live
   He whom to-day we cheer,—
Downing! the darling of Ninety-five,
   Captain and Pioneer.

IN THE SPIDER'S WEB.

(WRITTEN TO MUSIC.)

T was once upon a time,
That the hero of this rhyme,
Guileless Freshie, green as grass,
Met an artful Senior lass.
Oh, she smiled on him demurely,
She had loved none other, surely,
And her heart was his securely,—
Poor little maid!

For she had never seen the mau-
soleum,
By the stock-farm she had never
strayed,
She had never seen the Quad by
moonlight,—
Poor little Roble maid!

So this Freshman lent his aid,
Just to introduce the maid

To the beauties of the place,
But she set him such a pace
That he spent his monthly ration
All in ice-cream dissipation,—
Now he damns co-education
    And the Roble maid;
  For it was not quite true that

    She had never seen the mausoleum,
      Nor never near the stock-farm
      strayed;
    She knew each corner of the Quad
      by moonlight,—
    Sly little Roble maid!

"HONI SOIT QUI MAL Y PENSE."

т is said there is a maiden
    Living over in the Hall,
    Whose tender little spirit
      Several dreadful things appall,—
    Thro' whose modest, fluttering nature
Suddenly a shudder thrills
At the mention or the memory
    Of the recent Vaudevilles.

In the chapel she takes refuge
    From the naughtiness elsewhere,
Never dreaming that at one time
    We'd have doubtless held them there.
Little maiden, too incautious,
    Those suggestive colored bills
Should have given you suspicions
    Of the daring Vaudevilles.

Was it your sweet voice, we wonder,
    Pointing out excitedly,

"HONI SOIT QUI MAL Y PENSE."

In the ballet poster, evils
   That the others failed to see?
Oh, why did you, little maiden,
   With your dainty moral frills,
Ever brave the rank contagion
   Of those sinful Vaudevilles!

We have heard how sore they shocked you;
   And your high resolve is known,
Never to incur acquaintance
   With the baleful stars that shone.
Little maiden, be not anxious;
   While we have our own free wills,
You will never know the actors
   In those horrid Vaudevilles.

Wound up in your righteous wrappings
   For a life of cats and tea,
You need never dread disturbance
   From such common clay as we.
Let us go our way unhindered
   To pursue the pace that kills,
And, though forced to do without you,
   We will stick to Vaudevilles.

LORELEI.

H
E fareth in a joyous wise
　　Where runs the road 'neath gentle
　　　skies ; —
　　How should his canine heart sur-
　　　mise
That where the red-roofed towers rise
　　The blood is red upon the slab?
His way is warm with sunlight yet,
He knoweth not the sun must set;
And he hath in the roadway met
　　The Ladye of the Lab.

How should he read her face aright?
Upon her brow the hair is bright,
Within her eyes a tender light,
Her luring hands are lily-white,
　　Tho' blood be red upon the slab;
Her calling voice is siren-sweet,—
He crouches fawning at her feet,—

LORELEI.

(It is a fatal thing to meet
  The Ladye of the Lab!)

And she hath ta'en him with a string
To where the linnets never sing,
Where stiff and still is everything,
And there a heart lies quivering
  When blood is red upon the slab:
O little dog that wandered free!
And hath she done this thing to thee?
How may she work her will with me,—
  The Ladye of the Lab!

105

THE LAST GOOD-BY.

HE music is hushed in the night, boy,
    The crowds from the booths are
        gone,
The moon on the canvas is white,
        boy,
We stand in the Quad alone;
The lanterns that pointed the eaves, boy,
    Catch fire, blaze a moment, and die,
For it 's now that the Pioneer leaves, boy,—
    He has come to his last good-by.

I welcomed the fairy-like change, boy,
    For somehow it made me feel
Relieved that the place should seem strange, boy,—
    The heartache was all too real.
For a man cannot help feeling shame, boy,
    And yet I 'd have had to cry
If the old Quad had looked just the same, boy,
    When it came to the last good-by.

THE LAST GOOD-BY.

I told her good-night at the hall, boy,
    Where often I've said it before;
We knew 't was the end of it all, boy,
    The old walks would know us no more;
And still, though I 'll never forget, boy,
    That soft little parting sigh,
I knew in my heart that not yet, boy,
    Came the worst of this last good-by.

The girls are all right in their place, boy,
    And doubtless we both of us show
The power of a feminine grace, boy,
    That has bettered us both, we know;
But after these four glad years, boy,
    What co-ed attachment can vie
With the love of us two Pioneers, boy,
    In the Quad for our last good-by?

The fun and the folly of youth, boy;
    We have shared to the full, we two,—
The thirst of the heart after truth, boy,
    I have felt it and followed, with you;

And now the companionship ends, boy,
   The manifold meanings that lie
In the depths of the words, "college friends," boy,
   Make holy this last good-by.

To-morrow we go to the Gym, boy,
   And then we are done with it all;
I 'll warrant the place will be dim, boy,
   When we 've answered that last roll-call.
Then, here, with our hands gripped tight, boy,
   In the dear old Quad, you and I,
Let us tell it together, "Good-night," boy,
   God bless it forever,—Good-by!

THE STEM

THE ALUMNUS

AFTERWARD.

'VE left college and you 're still there,
　　Spending money while I am
　　　　saving,
　　But once in a while we two meet
　　　　where
The steps lead down from the city paving,
　And there we talk of the life each knows,
　　The sun and wind of the college weather;
We three friends, while the evening goes,
　　You and Pilsner and I together.

Pilsner 's a jolly, congenial chap,
　　Surnamed Schlitz, and found wherever
They keep the best of this world on tap,—
　　Sparkling always, unpleasant never;
And what if he really crossed the sea,
　　Or is native-born, who cares a feather,
So long as he makes our number three,
　　You and Pilsner and I together?

AFTERWARD.

I went out into life last May,
    Only a space, but it seems much longer,—
Change comes quick when one goes away,
    Pleasures weaken and cares grow stronger;
And so, when chatting again are we,
    I doubt a little and wonder whether
This means to you what it does to me,—
    You and Pilsner and I together.

IN THE COLD, COLD WORLD.

(WRITTEN TO MUSIC.)

E were jolly Pioneers
      Not so many moons ago,
   All the joys of Mayfield evenings
      We were said to fully know;
         But there came a day for leaving,
And the great world lay before,
So we packed our little schoolbooks,
   And we 'll use them never more.
      In the cold, cold world,
Ah, goodby to youthful follies,
   All those lazy days are o'er;
Bumming now must have cessation,
For just after graduation
Comes a painful revelation
   In the cold, cold world!

In those happy days we labored
   When we pleased, or not at all,

112

And we made a great impression
   On the world,—at Roble Hall.
Now we get a cold reception
   From the world we thought to win,—
When we ring her iron door-bell,
   We can never find her in.
     In the cold, cold world,
Things are very, very different,
   It is not the dear old Quad;
There the palm-trees gently rustle,
But outside it 's noise and bustle,
And it 's *we* who have to rustle
     In the cold, cold world!

AN OLD ACQUAINTANCE.

HEN back into the Quad I came
    In my alumnusship,
It did not wholly seem the same;
    The old companionship
    Was missing, and I longed to hear
Familiar accents in my ear,
    To feel a well-known grip.

The while I mourned this chilling change
    With trembling of the lip,
I heard a voice no longer strange,
    I felt a well-known grip,
And knew that Hodges' Dog was nigh,
And that he had not passed me by
    In my alumnusship.

WHEN WE COME BACK NO MORE.

WONDER, when from summer sleep
　　The old Quad wakes again,
When calling bells their vigils keep
　　And watch for us in vain,—
Those bells on which we heaped,
　　　　last year,
　Anathemas galore,
But now are grown so strangely dear
　When we come back no more,—

I wonder if among the leaves
　　A voice will whisper low,
A little dreaming voice that grieves
　　Over the long ago;
If new-filled places will forget
　　Who loved them best before,
Or stir a little with regret
　　That we come back no more.

WHEN WE COME BACK NO MORE.

When underneath the sacred shade
　　Where shines our name to-day,
With stranger steps the man and maid
　　Of '99 shall stray,
Will our old tree, bent down to hear
　　The same things o'er and o'er,
Forget this is not yester-year
　　And we come back no more?

Beyond the Palo Alto hills
　　The days slip stealthily;
The echo of their footsteps fills
　　The Quad with memory;
There where we made a painted boast,
　　The chapel site before,
Lies glimmering the twilight ghost
　　Of what will come no more.

We scatter down the four wide ways,
　　Clasp hands and part, but keep
The power of the golden days
　　To lull our care asleep,

116

And dream, while our new years we fill
    With sweetness from those four,
That we are known and loved there still,
    Though we come back no more.

www.ingramcontent.com/pod-product-compliance
Lightning Source LLC
Chambersburg PA
CBHW030630270326
41927CB00007B/1376